Adult Coloring Book Animals of the World Volume II

Copyright © 2016

For resale and distribution information, please contact us via www.booboone.com

Gypsy Vanner by Lena London

Groundhog by Lena London

Leopard

Raccoon

Red Panda by Lena London

Bushbaby

Sitting Cougar

Sheep

River Otter by Lena London

Silverback Gorilla

Lion by Lena London

Sloth hanging upside down

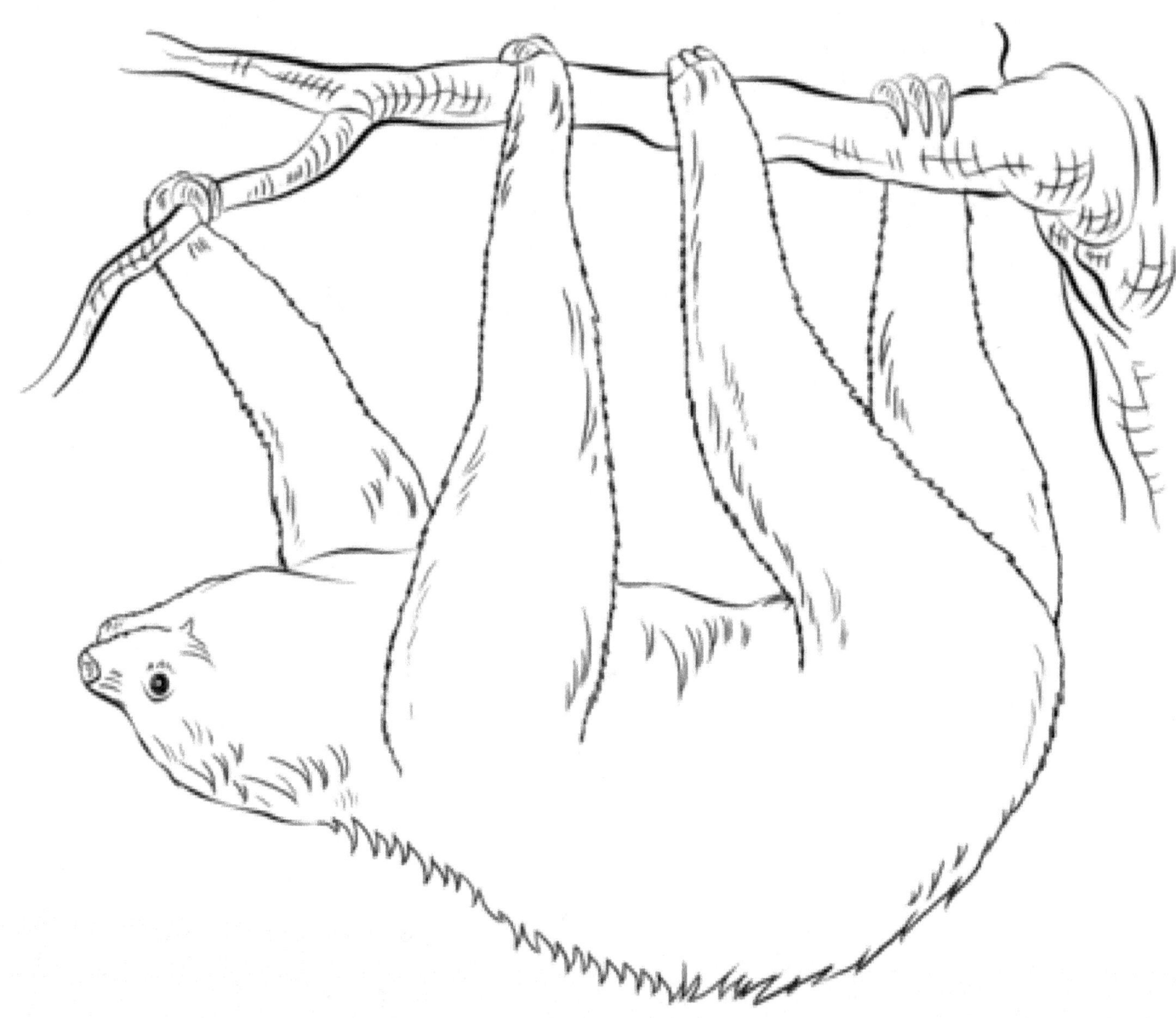

White-eared Opossum by Gennadiy Lukaynenko

Running Foal by Lona London

Icelandic Horse

Sumatran Tiger

Skunk by Lena London

Swedish Reindeer

Texas Longhorn

Two ponies grazing

White-tailed Deer

Wild Boar

Tamarin Monkey by Lena London

Yellow Mongoose by Delarno

Zebra

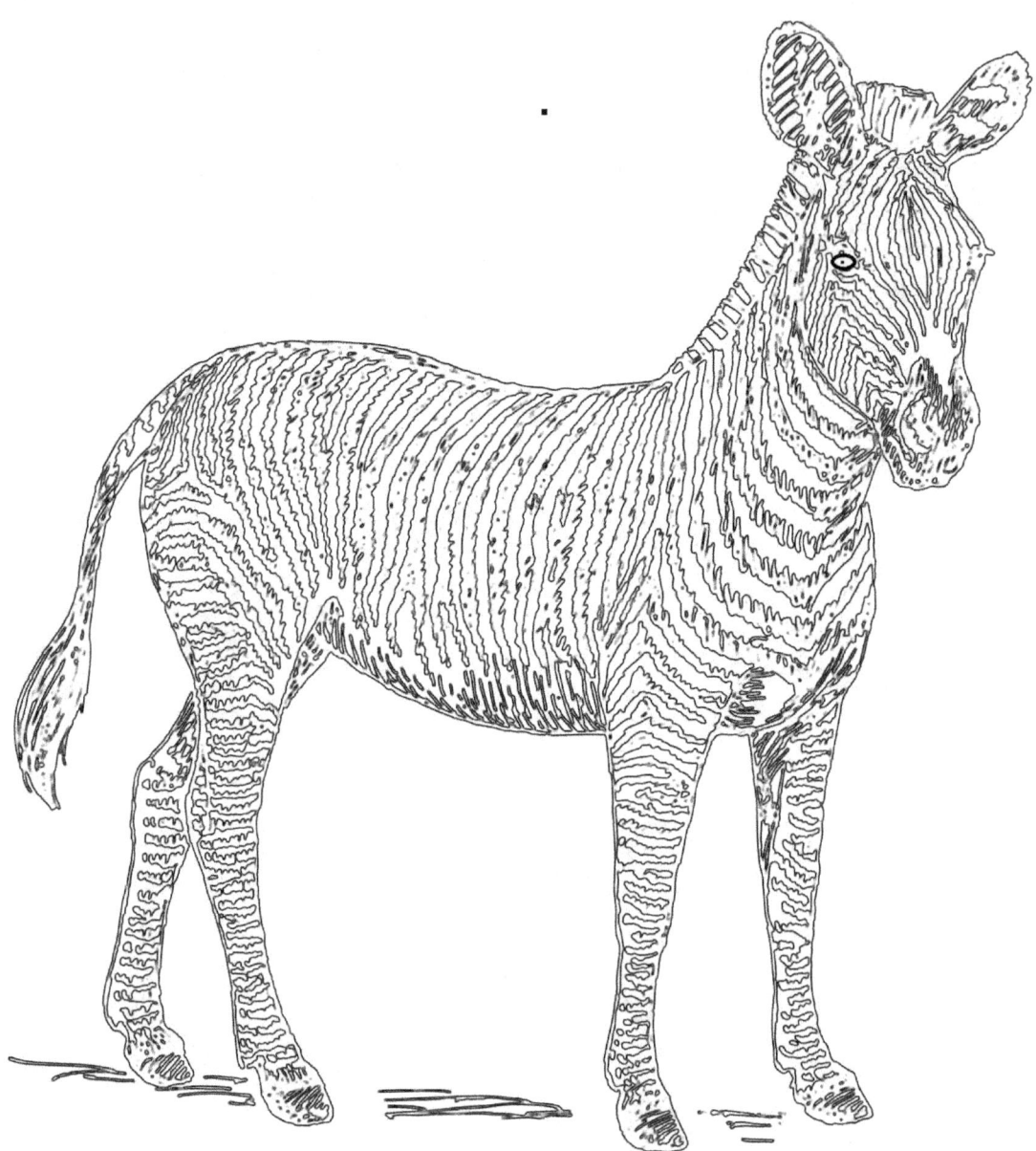

Cheetah

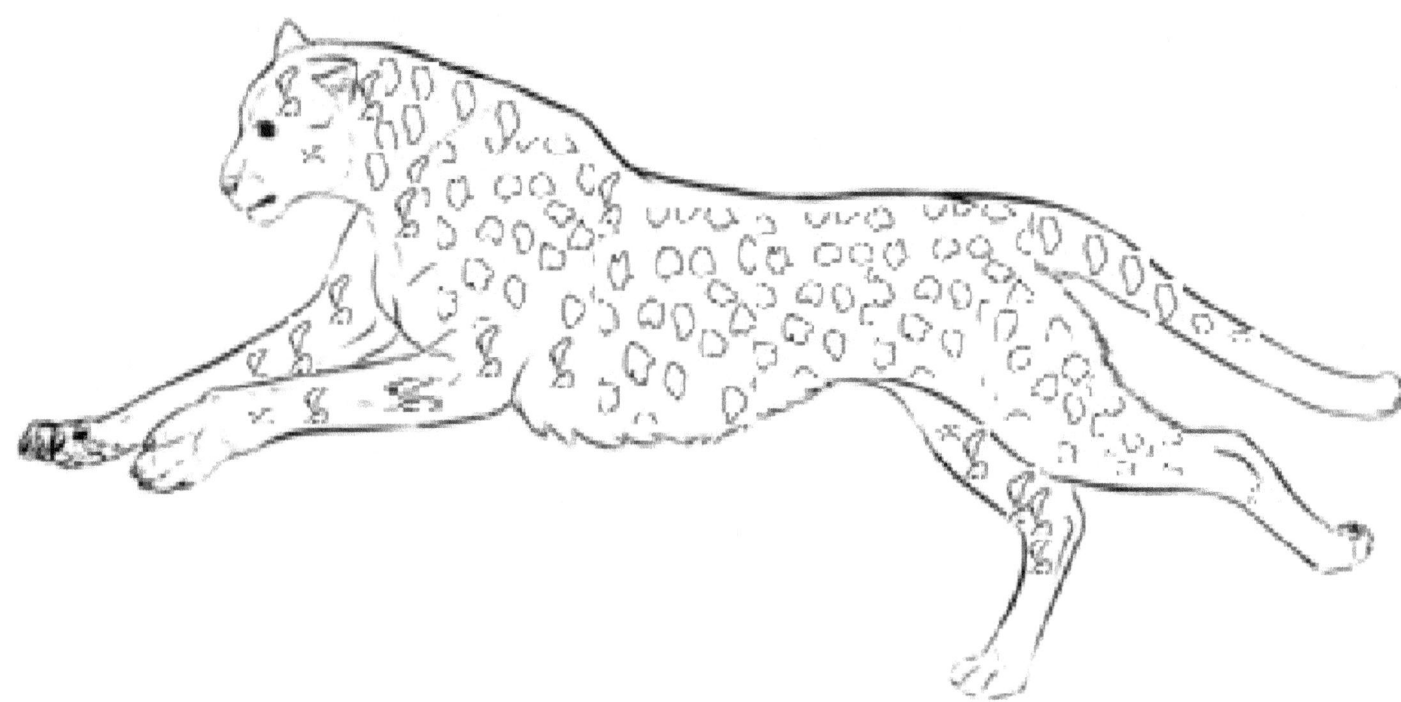

Bull Riding Rodeo

Grey Wolf

Striped Hyena by Gennadiy Lukaynenko

Walking Yak by Lena London

White Rabbit Standing

Alaskan Husky Dog

British Shorthair Cat

Aardvark by Lena London

African Rhino by Lena London

American Bison

Armadillo by Lena London

Baby Cougar

Black Panther

Black-footed Ferret by Lena London

Cow

Cougar by Gennadiy Lukaynenko

Canadian Lynx by Lena London

Coyote by Natalia Moskovkina

Fox

Baboon

Hippo by Lena London

Jackal by Lena London

Jaguar by Lena London

Warthog by Lena London

Camels